LUTON
IN
50
BUILDINGS

PAUL RABBITTS

AMBERLEY

To Helen Smith, who rarely ventures north of Luton

First published 2020

Amberley Publishing, The Hill, Stroud
Gloucestershire GL5 4EP

www.amberley-books.com

British Library Cataloguing in Publication Data.
A catalogue record for this book is available from the British Library.

ISBN 978 1 4456 9281 4 (print)
ISBN 978 1 4456 9282 1 (ebook)

Typesetting by Aura Technology and Software Services, India.
Printed in Great Britain.

Contents

Key

1. Parish Church of St Mary
2. Moat House, Moat Lane, Leagrave
3. The Former Cock Public House, No. 38 Park Street
4. Stockwood House Stable Block
5. Baptist Union Chapel, Castle Street
6. Central Block of St Mary's Hospital, Dunstable Road
7. High Town Methodist Church and Hall, High Town Road
8. Wheelwright Arms, No. 34 Guildford Street
9. Ceylon Baptist Church (The Spires), Adelaide Street
10. The Castle Public House (and former White Hart Public House), Castle Street
11. The former Fedora & Firkin Public House, No. 9 Chapel Street, Luton (previously the Griffin, then the Bitter End)
12. Ebenezer Chapel, Hastings Street
13. Christ Church, Upper George Street
14. Great Northern Public House, No. 63 Bute Street
15. No. 36 George Street (the former Bell Hotel)
16. Bute Mills
17. Seventh Day Adventist Church, No. 1 North Street
18. Luton Hoo
19. Former Boots and Hepworths, No. 27 George Street
20. Church of St Matthew, Wenlock Street
21. Wardown House, Park and Buildings
22. Former Hat Factory, No. 46 George Street
23. Former Plait Warehouse, No. 42 George Street
24. Former Chapel Langley School, Russell Street
25. Cowper Arms, No. 53 Cheapside
26. Bute House (formerly Bute Hospital)
27. Hibbert Cottages Almshouses
28. Former Hat Factory, No. 64 Bute Street
29. Former Liberal Club, Nos 11 and 13 Manchester Street
30. Former Hat Factory, No. 50 Guildford Street
31. Bailey Hill Water Tower and Hart Hill Water Tower
32. Bury Park United Reform Church
33. Former Hat Factory, No. 40 Guildford Street
34. Vauxhall Motors, Kimpton Road
35. Kenilworth Road, Home of Luton Town Football Club
36. Former Hat Factory, No. 37–39 Guildford Street
37. The Painters Arms, High Town Road
38. Stirling House, Former Hat Factory, No. 30 Guildford Street
39. The Hat Factory, No. 65–67 Bute Street
40. Paul Walser's Former Hat Factory, Midland Road
41. Denbigh High School, Alexandra Avenue
42. Church of St Andrew, Blenheim Crescent
43. Blue Rails, Old Bedford Road
44. Luton Town Hall
45. London Luton Airport
46. Former Bingo Hall and Odeon Cinema, No. 127 Dunstable Road
47. Former Cinema, No. 51 George Street
48. The Arndale Centre, Mall and Central Library
49. Luton Central Mosque, Westbourne Road
50. University of Bedfordshire Campus

Introduction

Many histories of Luton have been written and published over the years and it is not the intention of this book to repeat much of this. A number of these are referenced within 'Further Reading'. The purpose of this book is a celebration of Luton and its rich and varied built heritage.

Today, much of medieval Luton lies buried under the Arndale Centre and the Mall with street names such as Castle Street, Bridge Street and Mill Street an indication of the planning of the old town. There were markets and fairs and details of a religious fraternity. Markets and fairs continued into the life of Victorian Luton, which remained a thriving market town. A list of trades included brewing and malting, both important local industries. Thanks to the quality of local straw,

Originally this large industrial building on Leagrave Road was used by the Swedish ball-bearing manufacturer SKF, and their name can still be seen carved in the stonework at the top of the entrance portico. However, it was sold in 1978 and SKF now occupy premises in Sundon Park Road elsewhere in Luton. The building is now used for multi-occupancy business suites.

the town had already begun to be an important hat-making centre. The town was thriving and local people were looking to the future with the Gas and Coke Company and the Water Company becoming established.

Local leaders were afraid that the hat industry was a narrow base for prosperity in the town, so they advertised nationally to invite other industries into the area. This was very successful. Hayward Tylers arrived in 1871, Laporte Chemicals in 1898, Co-operative Cocoa and Chocolate Factory in 1902, British Gelatine Works in 1903, Commercial Cars in 1906, Davis Gas Stove in 1907, Kent's in 1908 and Skefko (SKF) in 1910. However, the most significant arrival was Vauxhall Motors, which came in 1905 and eventually played a huge part in the life of the town.

People were drawn to Luton because of its reputation as a place with low unemployment. Women and girls would come during the height of the hat-making season, swelling the population considerably. When other industries, such as Vauxhall Motors, established themselves, workers came from other parts of England and also Wales and Scotland. Irish labourers helped to build the M1 in the 1950s. When travel was easier there were many who came here from the Indian subcontinent and the West Indies. Then came the European Union and Luton welcomed new residents, for example from Poland. The diversity of the town was to change the town considerably, including its architecture and buildings.

Luton has been transformed beyond recognition since Victorian times due to the impact of the hat-making industry and the coming of Vauxhall Motors along with twentieth-century modernisation. What is apparent is the rich architectural heritage that was a direct result of the hat-making and straw-plaiting industry and the significant amount of factory units that were established, both large scale and domestic. However, such modernisation has come at a cost, and by delving into the built heritage of the town we discover the many magnificent buildings that have been lost, including the Corn Exchange, the Public Baths and Winter Assembly Hall, the Plait Halls and the Grand Theatre, all demolished to make way for the Arndale Centre. There are many lessons to be learnt here but most important is the need to preserve what remains. Luton has a fascinating history and despite what is often portrayed in the media, it is a town with a future and a town with some incredible architecture.

The 50 Buildings

The Parish Church of St Mary, one of the largest in Bedfordshire, is one of the finest examples of medieval churches in England and dates mainly from the fourteenth and fifteenth centuries. The earliest church here though was present in around 931 and was founded by King Athelstan as an act of thanksgiving for victory over the Danes. The church was handsomely endowed with the surrounding land owned by the king in Saxon and early Norman times.

The current building was established on a new site in approximately 1121 by Robert, Earl of Gloucester, but not consecrated until 1137. It was built by the Normans as a cruciform but without any aisles; however, a central tower was present. As the population increased, a south aisle was added in *c.* 1190 and a north aisle followed in *c.* 1230. The current arches from the transepts are the earliest dateable features present.

By the fourteenth century, further enlargements and additions were made with a tower added, transepts extended, and a vaulted sacristy with upper room built north of the chancel. Many further changes were made during the fifteenth century with significant rebuilding in the Perpendicular style. In 1461 Lord John Wenlock (whose family had been connected with the manor since 1389) rebuilt and extended Someries Chapel, with its big windows and magnificent double-arched stone screen. The sacristy was re-erected further east. Finally, the west tower was made taller and most windows renewed. All these changes give the building its grandeur and spaciousness appreciated today by so many.

Further restorations were commenced in 1865, this time initiated by the vicar, James O'Neill, with the tower restored in 1906 and the Wenlock Chapel in 1914. O'Neill was vicar for thirty-four years and was incredibly well liked by parishioners. Known as 'the galloping vicar', he travelled around his parish in a four-wheeled gig, drawn by a large black horse called Bessie. Not everyone was seen as a supporter of the local vicar however. Described by some as an 'odious bully', he was sued at least twice and on one occasion charged with assaulting his churchwarden. He was also incredibly intolerant of the nonconformists. Nevertheless, he is commemorated in the centre aisle of the church by the Revd James O'Neill pulpit, presented to the church in 1882 by his parishioners.

A number of other extensions were added in 1968, comprising of a hall, offices and vestry, which were planned to blend in with the magnificent old building.

Above: An early print of St Mary's Church.

Below: St Mary's Church, one of the best medieval churches in the country.

Stone carvings on
St Mary's Church.

The Wenlock Chapel contains several monuments, brasses and recessed tombs to members of the Wenlock and Rotheram families as well as many other memorials and details of note.

2. Moat House, Moat Lane, Leagrave

Sometime between 1370 and 1400, the Moat House at Leagrave was built. This was originally a residential hall consisting of a large hall separated from a bower by a cross passage. The walls were constructed of timber and wattle with a facing of brick and Totternhoe stone. The roof timbers in this building are still preserved and consist of decorated arch-braced collar beams. The original covering was thatched. Behind the existing house stood a courtyard with kitchens and stables ranged around it. The whole building was surrounded by a moat with rounded corners and may have been crossed by a drawbridge on the north side. The fourteenth-century hall was divided up into smaller rooms and floors somewhere around the beginning of the seventeenth century. Rather strangely, on the wall of the cellar was an inscription that has been scratched recording that on 23 July 1666, hailstones as big as cricket balls fell around the house.

The original house was more than likely built by the 'de Bereford' family, though the Ackworths lived there from around 1400 to 1548. John Ackworth was one of the founders of the Guild of the Holy Trinity in 1474, and a brass on the wall of the north transept of Luton church shows him with his two wives. Below this effigy are seventeen small figures who may represent eight brothers and nine sisters of the Guild of the Holy Trinity.

Local author, lecturer and historian James Dyer led a successful fight to save what is now the town's oldest building in the late 1960s. Plans to pull it down were scrapped and it was converted into a pub/restaurant, which it remains to this day.

The Old Moat House, one of Luton's oldest buildings.

3. The Former Cock Public House, No. 38 Park Street

The building at No. 38 Park Street was once The Cock public house and was listed in 1979. The building is certainly of interest as it is a two-storey timber-framed building of the seventeenth century or possibly even earlier origins, with the front rebuilt in red brick in the early nineteenth century, with an extension of one bay including a wagon-way to the left. A secondary two-storey timber-framed wing with straight bracing and lighter studding extends to the rear and is probably of late seventeenth-century build. This makes this building one of the oldest remaining secular buildings in Luton and therefore of considerable interest.

In his 1928 book *The History of Luton and Its Hamlets*, William Austin stated that the earliest mention of the Cock is 1671 and that in 1759 it was sold to an H. Bonner. The first mention of the public house though is not until 1822 and the first surviving countywide register of alehouse licences. William Austin states,

In 1828 a coach called 'The Times' started to run between Luton and London. In the coaching days, it was common for gentlemen themselves to horse coaches, and in this case Mr. Charles Austin senior horsed this coach for some years, and if he happened to be a passenger handled the 'ribbons'. More generally the coach was driven by Mr. Clarke of the Cock Inn.

William Austin continues,

> In 1828 Messrs, Frederick S. Burr, brewers in Park Street, sank a deep well
> on their premises. The depth of this was 465 feet, and in boring to that depth
> material was brought to the surface of the Lower Gault geological formation.
> From this Mr. Burr had a brick made and inscribed with the legend 'F. Burr,
> 465 feet, January 1828'. The brick was built into the wall of the Market Room in
> the Cock Inn, Park Street, the property of his firm. The depth of the boring was
> at that time considered a remarkable achievement.

In 1860, following the death of Frederick Burr, his brewery, along with all its
tied licensed houses, was conveyed to rival Luton brewer Thomas Sworder.
In 1897 Sworder sold his business to another rival Luton brewer, John
William Green, who, at the same time, turned his business into a limited company
under the name J. W. Green Limited. This firm remained owner of the Cock until
the company merged with Midlands brewers Flowers in 1954, the new company
taking the Flowers name. In 1962 Flowers was taken over by huge national
brewing concern Whitbread.

Thomas Sworder's uncle, also called Thomas Sworder, was guarantor for his
nephew's purchase of Burr's Brewery and, due to his nephew's mishandling of
his business, had to take an active interest in running it. In 1864 his lane agent,
Robert How, reported to him,

The former Cock Inn public house, with a very long history.

Mr. Lane [Samuel Lane, butcher, wheelwright and coach builder of Park Street] has commenced building against the Premises next the Cock Inn and I find that when he gets the Building up it will entirely exclude the light from the window lighting the Cock Staircase. I think you had better write him in time or send me a notice to serve on him before the Building proceeds any further, he has also taken up the drain which conveyed the water from the Cock Inn premises. Notice of this ought also to be given him.

Notice was duly served but Lane ignored it and continued to build. A second notice was served and this, too, was ignored. Frustratingly the end of the saga is not recorded in the correspondence.

Today the Cock is no longer a public house but has become an Italian restaurant.

4. Stockwood House Stable Block

The Crawley family were major landowners in Luton since the seventeenth century. There is reference to a Thomas de Crawley as far back as 1332. Later, Francis Crawley was made a judge to the court of Charles I. During the Civil War, the Crawleys and the Napier family took the Royalist side and their estates were confiscated and eventually returned to them after the execution of the king in 1649. Sir Francis Crawley died the same year. It was his descendant John Crawley who built Stockwood House, which was completed by 1740. The family continued to live here and by the 1930s Ross Skinner

Stockwood House, demolished in 1964.

Above: Stockwood House Stable Block.

Below: New building facilities at Stockwood Park.

Crawley was in residence. Soon after the outbreak of the Second World War, the house was converted to a hospital catering for children suffering with hip diseases. The patients were transferred by converted single-deck buses from the Bartholomew's Hospital at Swanley in Kent. It was considered to be too dangerous in that area because it was on the edge of the balloon barrage. However, Luton saw enemy activity due to the nearby motor works. Initially there was not any X-ray facility there, but one was added later and housed in the stable block. Before that installation, patients were taken by private car to nearby Luton and Dunstable hospital. The house was then named Alexandra Hospital for Children with Hip Disease.

Stockwood House was to eventually fall into disrepair and was sadly demolished in 1964. What remained were magnificent grounds that were opened to the public as a public park and municipal golf course. The stable block survived and was eventually opened as the Stockwood Museum and houses the Mossman Collection of horse-drawn vehicles. In 2008–09, the stable block was restored and extended with the Stockwood Discovery Centre added. Today, this centre in Luton is a popular family visitor attraction that includes the carriage museum, a number of themed and historic landscaped gardens, adventure play areas as well as galleries with local history collections and exhibitions.

5. Baptist Union Chapel, Castle Street

This impressive chapel was built between 1836–44 in neoclassical style with Greek Doric columns at the entrance. It has a very symmetrical exterior, and internally it is a typical nonconformist hall. The building was sold in 1986 and converted into flats. The east end of the chapel is wrapped round by a large Sunday school building of 1892, but was not included in the listing of the existing chapel.

January 1975 officially marked the beginning of Luton Central Baptist Church. The three town centre Baptist churches had voted overwhelmingly to amalgamate and form one fellowship. These three were Park Street Baptist (the oldest of the three, originally registered as 'Baptist Meeting House' in 1815), Union Chapel, Castle Street (which was founded in 1836 by members of Park Street and was originally a Union Church, but later became Baptist), and Ceylon Baptist in Wellington Street (this church was formed by people from both Park Street and Castle Street in 1846).

The original building in Park Street was demolished so that a new building could be erected to suit the needs of the new church fellowship. With services being shared between Wellington Street (morning) and Castle Street (evening) a building fund was set up, and approximately £500,000 would eventually have to be raised. The other two premises were later sold. Wellington Street is now a suite of offices known as 'The Spires' whilst the former Baptist Union Chapel on Castle Street is now Housing Association flats.

The Baptist Union Chapel on Castle Street, now flats.

With money raised and planning permission granted, work began in October 1985. The new building was completed, and a service was held to officially open it on 25 October 1986. The building, which remains on Castle Street in its neoclassical style, is far superior as a building compared to the current Luton Central Baptist Church.

6. Central Block of St Mary's Hospital, Dunstable Road

St Mary's Hospital was originally created from a workhouse located on Dunstable Road. Several of the original buildings still remain. Following the introduction of the National Health Service in 1948, the site became St Mary's Hospital and the central block of the main building became a care home for elderly people. It is now a Grade II listed building.

The hospital's origins lie wholly in the Luton Union Workhouse, which was built on land donated by the Marquis of Bute with the central block, designed by John Williams and opened in 1836. An infirmary block was eventually built to the west of the central block in the 1870s and was replaced by a new infirmary building to the north of the central block in 1912. After the medical facilities had absorbed the central block itself, the whole site became St Mary's Hospital in 1930 and it joined the National Health Service in 1948.

The main block was subsequently acquired by Bupa and substantially refurbished. It remains a care home for the elderly.

The former Luton Union Workhouse, once a hospital and now a care home.

7. High Town Methodist Church and Hall, High Town Road

Primitive Methodism arrived in Luton from Aylesbury in 1839. S. Turner and H. Higginson were the 'connexional pioneers' who were credited with the evangelising of Luton and Dunstable. The church developed so that in 1843 Luton was made into a separate circuit.

The 1851 religious census includes a return for High Town Primitive Methodist Chapel, Luton, made by Henry Pope, Minister, Wellington Street. The return states that the chapel had been erected in 1839 and contained 130 free sittings, 220 other sittings and fifty standing. However, Pope noted that 'Our religious Services were held in the Town Hall, our Chapel being too small.' As a result, in 1852, a new chapel was erected and was registered for worship by Thomas Bennett of Luton, grocer (trustee), on 15 December 1852. This chapel was registered again for worship on 14 December 1866 by William Kitchen, Hightown, Luton, minister and registered for marriages the following day.

In June 1867, High Town chapel, Luton, hosted the Primitive Methodist conference and a conference camp meeting was held in the town. Two processions were formed starting from High Town and Park Town chapels which met on Park Square where they were addressed by Revd R. Fenwick. The *Bedfordshire Times and Independent* estimated that 'there could not have been less than between 5,000 and 6,000 persons present'.

Above left: The High Town Methodist Chapel of 1852.

Above right: The High Town Primitive Methodist Chapel of 1897.

Although other Primitive Methodist chapels were built in Luton, a new chapel was built in 1897 at High Town adjoining the 1852 building, which became the Sunday school. Fundraising for the new chapel started in 1895. There were no fewer than three stone-laying ceremonies for the new chapel between April and November 1897. The contract value of the chapel was £2,566 and the contractor was Mr Parkins. The chapel, accommodating 900 people, was opened on 4 May 1898 by the mayor of Luton in a service led by the Superintendent Minister Revd Thomas Humphries. This chapel was registered for worship and marriages by Thomas Humphries, No. 74 Wenlock St, Luton, superintendent minister on 17 May 1898.

8. Wheelwright Arms, No. 34 Guildford Street

The 'Wheelwright Arms', built *c*. 1840, is one of the most distinctive buildings in this area. It is likely to date from *c*. 1840. It differs, being a public house, in that it has a wide central doorway to either side of which is a window with a central stone mullion. The most striking features are the heavily moulded stone hoods supported on brackets running above the windows and doorway – this incorporation of medieval revival elements is unique within the local conservation area.

The Wheelwright Arms, one of Luton's most popular public houses, dates from 1840.

In the middle of the nineteenth century, the owners of the pub also carried on the trades of wheelwright, bonnet blocker and herring curer. During the busy hat trade era, with high-loaded carts passing to and from the railway stations, it was not permitted to have a traditional hanging pub sign, so the tools of the wheelwright's trade, together with a cart wheel, were mounted flush on the façade.

9. Ceylon Baptist Church (The Spires), Adelaide Street

Now converted to offices, the former Ceylon Baptist Church and Hall, in Adelaide Street, was built in 1848 and is known now as The Spires. It was re-fronted in 1886 with a church hall added to the rear in 1908 by an architect called Barnes. The original chapel of 1848 consists of three bays, and is built of red brick with rubber-brick dressings and a three-bay buttressed screen front of 1886 when the church was slightly lengthened. Barnes's addition of the church hall in 1908 is in a competent Arts and Crafts style with lively colours including stained glass in pseudo cartouche and floral patterns.

Above: The former Ceylon Baptist Church.

Below: Now known as 'The Spires', the former Baptist Church is now offices.

10. The Castle Public House (and former White Hart Public House), Castle Street

As might be expected from its position in the old market place of the town, the Castle is one of Luton's oldest public houses. The current building is certainly mid-nineteenth century and is stucco-faced and has a Welsh slate roof. Previously, the public house was called the White Hart (then, briefly, Scruffy Murphy, before changing to the Castle).

Despite its nineteenth-century date, the White Hart may be a much older institution. A White Hart is recorded in Luton as early as 1733. This has always been a popular name for public houses, so it may not be on the exact site of the current public house, but the description that it abutted a property which itself abutted 'north on the common street from the marketplace to Cross pond' shows it was, at the very least, very close.

In 1778 Margaret, wife of Philip Hayward, was buried in Luton and the parish register describes them as being 'of the White Hart'. The establishment is listed in the first countywide registers of alehouse licences of 1882 to 1828 and in 1827 its owner, Thomas Carter, devised it in his will to his wife Ann. He died in 1829.

In 1872 the White Hart was put up for sale by auction by the trustees for sale under the will of Frederick Samuel Cleaver, deceased, along with eleven

The Castle public house.

The Castle and the Red Lion Hotel opposite. The Red Lion is described as a 'complex group of late nineteenth-century and Edwardian buildings', and 'is in florid Edwardian style'.

other licensed premises. It was described as a 'brick-built House in a capital position, containing Good Bar, Bar Parlor [sic], Taproom, Kitchen, Cellar, Private Sitting Room and Five Bedrooms. A Large Yard in rear (with entrance in common with occupiers of adjoining premises), containing a brick and slated Store with Room over, a brick and tiled 4-stall Stable and Loft, a Printing Office adjoining, let to Mr. O'Doherty at £8 per annum, a Store and Stable let to Mr. Chamberlain at £8, a Store or Stale adjoining, and an open fronted Cart Lodge. The sub-tenant, Thomas George Edwards paid £1 per week rent. The property was leasehold and was leased by Cleaver for 21 years from Christmas 1869 at a rent of £80 per annum.' Unfortunately, the particulars do not reveal who bought the property.

Surprisingly, the buyer in 1872 was not John William Green, whose Phoenix Brewery in Park Street West was just a stone's throw from the White Hart, although his firm did own land at the rear of the building and it also owned the adjoining property, No. 3 Castle Street. This building was also the headquarters of the Luton Wine Company, founded by Green's rival Luton brewer Thomas Sworder and sold to Green with the rest of Sworder's business in 1897.

Today the Castle remains a popular public house.

11. The former Fedora & Firkin Public House, No. 9 Chapel Street, Luton (previously the Griffin, then the Bitter End)

The building at No. 9 Chapel Street is now no longer a public house but its history indicates that this has been its primary use. Now Grade II listed, it is described as a building that was an early nineteenth-century public house with very high-quality brick detailing.

The first mention of the establishment is in 1858 when Thomas Sworder of Hertford, uncle and business partner of Thomas Sworder of Luton, stated in a letter to Frederick Burr's executors, 'I propose to borrow £10,000 including the £2,500 now paid this day on security of the Crown, the Black Swan & the Griffin Public Houses.' This indicates that the Griffin had either been built by Sworder himself or had been a public house attached to the brewery of Frederick Burr, which the Sworders were in the process of acquiring (negotiations had opened in 1857 and the final conveyance would be 1860).

Thomas Sworder's business was adversely affected by purchasing Burr's brewery and for most of the rest of its existence hovered close to bankruptcy. In 1897 Sworder decided to retire and put his business up for sale. It was purchased by Luton rival John William Green, who immediately floated his company as J. W. Green Limited.

No. 9 Chapel Street, empty and virtually derelict.

Previous uses include a public house and nightclub but it is now looking for a new lease of life.

In 1954 J. W. Green Limited merged with Midlands brewery Flowers and the new company adopted the Flowers name. In 1962, the company was taken over by Whitbread. By 1995 the Griffin had been renamed The Bitter End and was to be renamed once more, to the Fedora & Firkin on its sale to the Firkin Brewery of Burton-on-Trent, Staffordshire, part of the Allied Domecq Group, in 1996. The pub, along with many others in the chain, brewed its own real ale. The Fedora & Firkin's microbrewery closed in 1999 with the sale of the Allied Domecq licensed houses to Punch Taverns. By 2006 the pub had become a nightclub. In June 2010, the building was up for sale. Today the building is empty and without use and in very poor condition.

12. Ebenezer Chapel, Hastings Street

The Ebenezer Chapel is a real surprise as one almost stumbles across it, hidden way on Hastings Street. Yet, when discovered, it is an imposing building in its own right. It was built in 1853 at a cost of £950, to accommodate a growing congregation of Particular Calvinistic Baptists. Not long after it was completed, a school hall was added to the rear of the chapel, where local children would gather to attend bible classes on Sunday afternoons. Morning and evening services were regularly hosted by Pastor Arthur Cook with often more than 500 worshippers present.

Above: The Ebenezer Chapel, tucked away in the backstreets of Luton.

Left: The fine stucco finish of the Ebenezer Chapel on Hastings Street.

Reformed Baptists (sometimes known as Particular Baptists or Calvinistic Baptists) are Baptists that hold to a Calvinist soteriology. They can trace their history through the early modern Particular Baptists of England. The first Reformed Baptist church was formed in the 1630s. For many years there had been a flourishing Baptist community in nearby Kensworth as early as 1689, but this was eventually to break off after an internal dispute that led to Luton members to divide off and form their own church. The church flourished under the leadership of Thomas Marsom, a well-respected member of an established family of merchants and shopkeepers. Nonconformists remained a minority in Luton throughout the seventeenth and eighteenth centuries but grew significantly in the nineteenth century. As the town expanded, many new chapels appeared such as the Ebenezer with the nonconformists promoting reliability, sobriety, honesty, hard work, good stewardship, punctuality and self-discipline. These were values that were appreciated in Luton's growing industry.

Today, the chapel remains a hidden gem among the streets of Luton, in its restrained neoclassical style.

13. Christ Church, Upper George Street

From the outset, this compact mid-nineteenth century church by architect H. Elliott (1856–60, 1864) and over extended by G. Vialls (1881) was beset by financial and structural problems. Erected on the corner of Dunstable Road and

An early view of Christ Church on Upper George Street.

Above left: The reduced spire of Christ Church, the building now home to offices.

Above right: Christ Church and its impressive tower with much-reduced spire.

Left: Christ Church, Upper George Street.

Upper George Street, the foundation stone was laid in 1856 by Mrs J. Crawley of Stockwood and the first services were held the following year. Unfortunately, the foundations were dug in clay, causing subsidence which necessitated rebuilding. Buttresses were added to the tower and eventually the spire was reduced in height. In 1861 a grand bazaar was held at the Old Brewery in Park Street, to clear debts incurred in the church's construction. Christ Church became the second independent parish of Luton after St Mary's. Today the building is used as high-quality offices.

14. Great Northern Public House, No. 63 Bute Street

The Great Northern has been listed as Grade II since February 1981, and of special interest. The building dates to the 1860s and is built of Luton grey bricks with yellow-brick quoins and a Welsh slate roof. The house was named after the Great Northern Railway station, which opened in Bute Street in 1858. This station was originally run by the Luton, Dunstable and Welwyn Railway Company. It was Luton's first station (the second, in Midland Road, following in 1868). The company was taken over by the Great Northern Railway Company in 1861.

The Great Northern public house, now a free house.

It may be that the Great Northern was originally called the Ship. In the book *Pubs and Pints* on Luton licensed premises by Stuart Smith, he states that this was the case. The Ship was also in Bute Street and the Ship and the Great Northern do not overlap in directories. The countywide licensing register of 1876 states that the Ship was owned by Saint Albans [Hertfordshire] brewers Adey and White. However, the register is often misleading on this point, frequently quoting breweries holding leases from private individuals as being the owners. In 1921 the Great Northern, along with four other public houses, was conveyed by Colonel Harvey Alexander and others to Benskins Watford Brewery Limited, as many were of the time. This indicates that the pub was in private ownership at this point. The Alexander family also owned the Cardinal public house in Brache Street.

By 1917, Arthur Walker Merry, who was responsible for carrying out inspections of a number of Luton public houses for the licensing magistrates, wrote of the Great Northern, 'This is a house containing Private Bar, Public Bar and Tap Room all with good supervision catering for the same class of trade as the Cooper's Arms.'

Benskins was eventually taken over by Ind Coope in 1957. That firm merged with two other breweries to form Allied Breweries in 1961. The pub is now a free house.

15. No. 36 George Street (the former Bell Hotel)

Luton had two establishments named The Bell, which were both located in George Street and at least one of which is first mentioned at a very early date. One, later called The Old Bell, lay on the west side of George Street, at the junction with Chapel Street, the other on the east side.

This building is the one on the east side of the street. The deeds to the building go back as far as 1641. The building was described as a capital *messuage*, meaning that it was large and of high status. It was described as 'abutting the street from The George to the Market Place'.

Surviving photographs of this building show a property that looks as if it was built around the middle of the nineteenth century and presumably at that time the building was extended forwards onto the road following the purchase of what was originally a butcher's shop. The likeliest date for this new building was between 1861 and 1864. Directories up to 1861 refer to this as the Bell Inn; those from 1864 described it as the Bell Commercial Hotel. The property was purchased by Thomas Sworder in 1860, which probably prompted this change.

In 1808 the Bell was conveyed to Luton brewers William and Jonathan Burr and by 1811 William Burr was in sole ownership of the brewery in Luton. He was succeeded by Solomon, Frederick and Charles. Frederick was the last survivor, dying in 1856. His executors sold his business to another Luton brewer, Thomas Sworder, in 1860 after protracted negotiations. This purchase, together with unwise speculation, nearly bankrupted Sworder and his business would lack firm financial foundations for most of the rest of its history. In 1897 he sold his brewery and its licensed houses to Luton rival John William Green.

The property occupying George Street today is not the same as that shown in photographs at the end of the nineteenth century. However, it was clearly built as the Bell since the name still occupies a stone pediment at the top of the frontage. The style of building seems to suit the beginning of the twentieth century and so, as Sworder built a new Bell shortly after buying it in 1860, so Green may have done the same after his purchase of 1897. The new building did not function as a hotel for very long. It is listed in *Kelly's Directory* for Bedfordshire of 1928 but by the time of the next *Kelly's* for the county, in 1931 the Bell is no longer listed, implying that it closed between these two dates. This is confirmed by the fact that *Kelly's* for 1931 lists G. & A. Pryce Limited, costumiers, at No. 36 George Street. By the time of the *Luton News Directory* of 1939 the premises were divided between Meakers Limited, outfitters, at No. 36 and Pryce at No. 36a.

Other directories for Luton show the following changes of use: by 1950 Meakers are still at No. 36 and Pryce at No. 36a but there is now a No. 36b, occupied by Brown & Green Limited (Social & Athletic Club). By 1960 Meakers occupy No. 36 and 'Paige, gowns' are at No. 36a. By 1972 Willerby Tailoring has replaced Meakers and, at the date of the last *Kelly's* for Luton, 1975, Willerby remains at No. 36 and Paige at No. 36a. Today its use is mixed retail.

The former Bell Hotel, but not a hotel for very long.

16. Bute Mills

During the last quarter of the nineteenth century the area close to the railway station emerged as a commercial and industrial hub. Coal and goods yards were established to the south of the Great Northern station and the section of Bute Street closest to them witnessed intense industrial development. Notably, in the late 1870s, this included the W. Dixon Engineering Works (rebuilt as the Bute Mills) and the Great Northern Steam Mills, so called because of their proximity to the Great Northern railway station. Despite recent demolition and refurbishment in the area, the core of the Great Northern Steam Mills does survive, but in a much-altered form.

Principal amongst the building though are the Bute Mills, which were built on the site of the Dixon works. It is one of the most recognisable buildings in the current area, constructed to a high standard using red brick and four storeys high. The most distinctive element of the building is, however, the iron water tank built on a corbelled brick support. This is a landmark feature, visible from a number of locations across the town centre and is emblazoned with 'Brown Bros', an important milling family long-established in Luton.

A former industrial building, now an important asset to the community of Luton.

Above left: Brown Bros emblazoned on the iron water tank.

Above right: Bute Mills and Stirling House – remnants of Luton's most important industrial heritage.

Today, Bute Mills is one of the most iconic buildings in Luton and it is a rare survivor of the town's built heritage following wholesale redevelopment of the town centre in the 1960s. Although the building had been refurbished in the 1990s as light industrial or office accommodation, it had lain empty for a number of years until it was purchased in 2013 by Youthscape. Like any unused building, it was at the time vulnerable to arson and vandalism. Without any obvious end use until the charity became involved, there was a further risk of ongoing redundancy and decay.

Youthscape undertook a fundraising campaign to purchase the building once it had identified it as a suitable base. The then owner agreed to sell for a fixed price and allowed the charity sufficient time to raise the funds. The £3.2 million restoration was funded by a number of charitable trusts and foundations.

In spring 2016, Bute Mills reopened as a UK centre of excellence to support the emotional and physical well-being of vulnerable young people.

17. Seventh Day Adventist Church, No. 1 North Street

The North Street Wesleyan Methodist church was built in 1871 and was originally part of the Luton Wesleyan Circuit. The chapel was on the other side of the street and virtually opposite the later chapel and cost £500 to build. By

1880 the chapel had joined the newly formed Waller Street Wesleyan Circuit but by 1913 the decision had been taken to sell the old chapel, which was no longer deemed adequate and there was the 'necessity of providing a more commodious building'. It was hoped that the old building would fetch £500 or £600.

At the same time application was made to erect a new chapel. It was hoped that it would accommodate 660 and the site had already been secured; it measured 70 feet by 80 feet and, at that time, contained six cottages. The new chapel was intended to measure 69 feet long by 48 feet wide and was expected to cost £3,530.

In 1932, the Wesleyan Methodists came together with the Primitive and United Methodists to form The Methodist Church of Great Britain. The following year the five Luton circuits (two Wesleyan and three Primitive) were amalgamated into two – Luton Circuit and the largely ex-Primitive High Town Circuit. North Street was part of the Luton Circuit.

In 1959, the decision was taken to close the church and sell the premises. Luton Borough Council would allow industrial use for two years otherwise the building would have to be used for worship or the site for private housing. The buildings were valued at £5,000. In December that year representatives of the

The Seventh Day Adventist Church on North Street.

Seventh Day Adventist Church offered £5,500 but the Methodists felt that £8,000 would be a better offer. The former chapel, along with Bailey Hill, was then offered at auction but there was no buyer. Eventually the Seventh Day Adventists increased their offer to £6,000 and the conveyance finally took place in November 1960 with the building's future secure.

18. Luton Hoo

There has been a house on the present site of Luton Hoo since at least 1601 when Robert Napier bought the estate. Today's mansion house dates from 1767 when it was the seat of the 3rd Earl of Bute, then Prime Minister to George III, and was designed by leading architect Robert Adam. However, instead of a new mansion, the earl got a heavily remodelled house. A fire interrupted works in 1771, but by 1774 the house, despite being incomplete, was inhabited. Dr Samuel Johnson visited in 1781 and spoke of the house's glory: 'This is one of the places I do not regret coming to see ... in the house magnificence is not sacrificed to convenience, nor convenience to magnificence.' Famous landscape designer Capability Brown was engaged to redesign the surrounding parkland and gardens, which now extend to 1,065 acres. Luton Hoo was reputedly one of his first commissions.

The house stayed rather the same until the early decades of the nineteenth century when the 2nd Marquis of Bute had Sir Robert Smirke – who designed

Luton Hoo, an early postcard view.

the British Museum and Eastnor Castle – draw up plans for a new Palladian west front (now the front of the property) in 1825. He desired a portico with wings and bows that reflected the east wing of Adam's design and completion of the frontage that Adam didn't see completed.

A fire gutted the mansion's interior in 1843, and seemingly discouraged, the marquis sold the estate to John Shaw-Leigh, who was a solicitor from Liverpool. Shaw-Leigh, on the advice of Smirke's younger brother, restored the house, except for the north wing, which was left as a shell. His son, John Gerrard-Leigh, took on the project of finishing the house in 1873, adding a chapel by architect George E. Street. This chapel was destroyed in 1940. His death in 1875 saw the estate pass to his widow, whose next husband let Luton Hoo to Sir Julius Wernher in 1900, and agreed to sell it in 1903. Sir Julius Wernher was a leading diamond dealer who commissioned Charles Mewes and Arthur Davis, the architects of the Ritz Hotel in London, to redesign the interior of Luton Hoo in a lavish Edwardian 'Belle Époque' style. After the death of Sir Julius, Harold Wernher inherited the estate from his father.

During the Second World War, the estate and mansion house was commissioned by Eastern Command and played an important role in wartime operations testing tanks before they were taken off to depots for war service.

Luton Hoo, the current house dating from 1767.

A fine setting for some of our greatest film and TV epics.

The magnificent façade of Luton Hoo.

On 26 June 1948, Sir Harold Wernher and his wife, Lady Zia, Countess Anastasia Mikhailovna de Torby, hosted a memorable visit by Sir Winston Churchill when 110,000 people gathered to hear him address the crowd and thank them for their support during the Second World War. Sir Harold and Lady Zia decided to exhibit Sir Julius's art collection within the house in 1951, including several items of the now famous Fabergé collection. They also bred several well-known racehorses including Brown Jack, who won twenty-five races in his ten-year racing career and Charlottown, who won The Derby in 1966.

Sir Harold died in 1973 followed by Lady Zia in 1977, with the estate passing to their elder grandson, Nicholas Phillips, who together with his wife developed the living accommodation into facilities for corporate functions and filming, to support the maintenance of the art collection.

The house has been a very popular location with television and film-makers, being used for films such as *Four Weddings and a Funeral*, *Enigma*, *Eyes Wide Shut*, *Inspector Morse*, *Nicholas Nickleby*, *Vanity Fair* and *Bleak House* to name but a few.

Following Nicholas Phillips' death in 1991 the estate was put up for sale in 1997 and was finally purchased by Elite Hotels in 1999. The hotel opened in October 2007 following an investment of more than £60 million and a painstaking restoration programme.

19. Former Boots and Hepworths, No. 27 George Street

One of the more attractive and unusual buildings is on the corner of George Street and Chapel Street. No. 27 George Street was first listed in a directory in 1871 when George Pigott, butcher, was in occupation. He is listed as being somewhere in George Street in directories of 1854, 1864 and 1869 and before that, in 1839, 1847 and 1850, a Francis Pigott is listed as a butcher in George Street. It seems at least plausible that the Pigotts had occupied No. 27 George Street as a butcher's shop since at least 1839. George Pigott was still at the premises in 1877 but by 1885 it was Arthur Pigott, who is last listed in *Kelly's Directory* for 1898. By the time of the directory for 1903 Boots Cash Chemist (Eastern) Limited was in occupation.

A plaque on the Chapel Street return frontage indicates that the current premises was built in 1915. The other date on the frontage indicates that something was established in 1874, although what this refers to is a mystery as it cannot apply to the Pigotts or subsequent occupiers Boots (founded 1849) or Hepworths (founded 1864).

By 1928, No. 27 George Street was owned as well as occupied by Boots. At this time, the building contained a basement store as well as a boiler house with a ground-floor that had a frontage to George Street and a return frontage to Chapel Street. The public area was a 'fine shop' with a gallery, whilst the yard outside was covered by glass. The first floor contained the fancy-goods showroom as well as a lavatory. The second floor contained three stockrooms

Above: The former Boots store and a very imposing building that almost looks out of place on George Street.

Below: Elaborate decoration overlooking George Street.

The Chapel Street frontage of the former Boots store.

and also a tearoom, a cloakroom, lavatory and store. The valuer's overall comments at the time were, 'Modern building, first class showrooms and Elevation, very attractive, fine corner site.'

Boots continued to occupy the building until at least 1960, *Kelly's Directory* for Luton of 1965 indicating that the premises were then vacant. By 1968 J. Hepworth Limited, tailors, which had occupied No. 47 George Street since 1903, were in occupation and were still there at the time of the last *Kelly's* for Luton in 1975. The current occupier is estate agent Taylors.

2C. Church of St Matthew, Wenlock Street

Built between 1875–76 by architect G. Vialls, the Church of St Matthew is a simple and dignified Early English-style building. The original church on this site was an old wooden building that had been brought from Woburn in 1873. The foundation stone of St Matthew's, the current church, was laid by the Duchess of Bedford in 1875 and the first service was held in December the following year. Inexpensive by today's standards, it cost £5,500 to erect and had seating for 1,000 people. During the First World War, church parades were a regular feature of St Matthew's, being attended by troops billeted nearby.

Above: The Church of St Matthew, opened in 1876.

Below: The Church entrance almost hidden by tree foliage.

21. Wardown House, Park and Buildings

The principal park in Luton is Wardown Park and it has a significant history. During the mid-nineteenth century the parcel of agricultural land known as Bramingham Shott lay with several adjacent similar small parcels bounded by the Old and New Bedford Roads, in open country to the north of Luton. In 1847 Robert How built a white stucco farmhouse on one of the plots towards the north of the area, which became known as Bramingham Shott. In 1868 Frank Chapman Scargill (1836–1919), a successful local solicitor, bought Bramingham Shott and began to buy up the adjacent parcels of land to the north and south whilst living in the farmhouse and planning his new mansion to be built on the site of, or close to, the existing house. In 1875 Scargill commissioned architect C. T. Sorby to design and build a new house, which was completed by 1877, having cost £10,000, with a similar amount having been spent on other estate buildings, including lodges. Gardens and pleasure grounds were laid out around this building, and further features including a park were added during the 1880s and early 1890s.

In 1894 Scargill retired and moved away from Luton, and in 1897 the estate was leased to B. J. H. Forder, who eventually changed the name to Wardown House after his former home in Buriton, Hampshire. In 1900, the estate was let to Mr Halley Stewart, founder of the London Brick Company, and in 1902 Scargill put it up for sale. It was not sold and in 1904 local councillors Asher Hucklesby and Edwin Oakley purchased the property for £16,250 on behalf of Luton Corporation and

Wardown Park and the original bandstand.

BANDSTAND, WARDOWN PARK, LUTON

Above: An early Edwardian view of Wardown House.

Below: Restored by National Lottery funding through Luton Borough Council, Wardown House is a popular museum today.

Above: The main entrance into Wardown House.

Below: A quaint thatched summerhouse in Wardown Park, built in *c.* 1876.

Above: One of the park lodges into Wardown Park.

Below: Wardown Park bowls pavilion, a wonderful example of 'parkitecture'.

over the following years the council spent a further £6,000 laying out new features. Hucklesby went on to be mayor of Luton. The pleasure gardens at Wardown Park were opened in 1905, and the remainder of the park was opened in 1906. From 1904 to 1907 a network of paths was laid out, a small lake with an island and boathouse was enlarged to incorporate further boating facilities, new bowling greens were laid out, and a bandstand erected. A cricket ground which Scargill had laid out was enlarged, incorporating the adjacent kitchen gardens, which were demolished.

It was always Hucklesby's dream that the house would eventually become a museum that would be 'interesting as well as of an educational nature'. Sadly, the house itself had been badly neglected and suffered from dry rot and Luton Council could not immediately afford the renovations. It remained empty for many years until it became a military hospital during the First World War. After the war, rooms were let to council employees with a café opening on the ground floor. The museum eventually opened in 1930, fulfilling Hucklesby's vision, having moved from the Carnegie Library where it started in 1927. At first the museum displays were held in just two rooms, but over the years it has filled the entire house. Restored again in 2017–18, the museum is once again the centrepiece of this impressive public park.

The park has a number of fine features including the Daisy Chain wall named because of the attractive brick pattern that features along the length of it. Believed to have been built around 1905, the wall was part of the original gardens of Wardown House before it was made into a public park. Other features include a quaint thatched summerhouse built in *c.* 1876 and a mock timber-framed park lodge dated *c.* 1878.

22. Former Hat Factory, No. 46 George Street

No. 46 George Street was first listed in a directory of 1877 when Hucklesby, Asher and Company, straw hat and bonnet manufacturers, were in occupation. By 1885 the occupants were listed as Asher Hucklesby and Arthur Panter, and, by 1903, A. Hucklesby and Company.

A trade catalogue of around 1890 curiously lists 'A. Hucklesby & Co - Straw Hat Manufacturers and Plait Merchants' at No. 42 George Street as well as Bond Street. The entry reads,

A premier position can be unhesitatingly accorded to the old-established house of Messrs. A. Hucklesby & Co. in reviewing the straw-hat trade of Luton. The business carried on by this well-known firm embraces that of the manufacture of all varieties of straw hats and bonets, and in addition they are extensive importers of and dealers in plait. The premises utilised front to George Street, and extend a long distance to Bond Street, being three stories in height, and of by no means unattractive appearance. They are most conveniently arranged throughout to suit all requirements of the business, the showrooms for finished goods and the store rooms for plait being excellently appointed, roomy and well-lighted.

The productions of this firm in all the innumerable styles, colours and varieties of straw hats and bonnets maintain a standard reputation in the trade, and are unsurpassed for beauty of finish, brightness of colour, and durability. That they keep pace with the prevailing fashions is evident from the splendid connections maintained. Messrs. Hucklesby & Co. give constant employment to a great number of hands, and they are in the most favourable position to meet the heaviest demands on the shortest notice. They hold an extensive stock of English and foreign plait, and in this branch of the business do a very large local and foreign trade. The business is certainly conducted throughout on the best lines, and under its present management it cannot fail to still further gain in value and importance. The firm have offices and sample rooms in all the principal continental cities.

By 1928, No. 46 George Street was still owned and occupied by A. Hucklesby & Company Limited, which also had premises at No. 48 George Street and Guildford Street. The firm also had premises on the south-east side of Bond Street, behind No. 44 George Street. Overall the valuer of the time commented, 'Built as Warehouse - good but not new.'

Hucklesby is last listed in 1931 and by 1950 the occupier was F. W. Woolworth Limited, which had previously been at No. 51 George Street. This firm was listed at the address as late as 1972. The last *Kelly's Directory* for Luton, 1975, has no listing for the premises at all.

A former straw and hat manufacturer, yet today, its former grandeur is lost among fast-food outlets.

23. Former Plait Warehouse, No. 42 George Street

No. 42 George Street is first mentioned in a directory of 1877 when Alfred William Linsell, 'English and Chinese plait warehouse', was in occupation. A commercial catalogue for Bedfordshire from around 1890 has an entry for A. W. Linsell:

> Formerly Luton and its vicinity employed thousands of persons, chiefly women and children, in plaiting straw for the manufacture of hats, bonnets, etc. This number is annually decreasing, although the trade is still advancing both in importance and extent. The reason is that vast quantities of the requisite plait are now imported from Shanghai and Chefoo, the principal centres of collection in China, which supplies us with immense quantities of well-made plait at a cheap rate. Some kinds of English plait are always in fair demand both for home and America, and the plaiters are paid from 3d. to 2s. per score for ordinary qualities and occasionally much higher prices for superior grades. Mr. A. W. Linsell, who is a merchant and also a manufacturer of straw goods, for both home and export, has, for many years, occupied a prominent place amongst the plait merchants and manufacturers of the town of Luton. This gentleman occupied spacious three-storied premises at the corner of George Street and Bond Street, which have a very large total frontage, and include two chief departments, one of

Yet another hat and bonnet manufacturer, its industrial past overtaken by more downmarket uses.

No. 42 George Street, an excellent example of where finer architecture is above the 'tacky' additions of shop frontages below.

which is devoted to straw plait in all its various grades of size, texture, colour, or quality, while the other is for goods manufactured therefrom, a good number of outworkers depending upon Mr. Linsell to take their produce. A very extensive trade is done by Mr. Linsell, who is always well to the front in all markets. He holds large and vaulable stocks of merchandise, and is in every way deserving of a conspicuous place in these pages.

By 1903 the business had become J. J. Linsell and Company. The firm remained there until at least 1928. *Kelly's Directory* for 1928 is the last to list J. J. Linsell and Company at No. 42 George Street. The directory for 1939 notes Marks and Spencer, which owned and occupied next door, No. 40 George Street, as occupier. Marks and Spencer continued in occupation until 2010 when they moved into the Arndale Centre.

24. Former Chapel Langley School, Russell Street

The impressive Chapel Langley Board School, on Russell Street, was built as a result of the Education Act of 1870. The act stated that any area which voted for it could have a school board. These new board schools could charge fees but they were also eligible for government grants and could also be paid for out of local government rates. Boards provided an education for the five to ten age group. A fine part of the building is a number of roundels, which are set in a red-brick and stone arch with the tympanum decorated with a moulded terracotta scallop pattern.

Chapel Langley School.

25. Cowper Arms, No. 53 Cheapside

Built in 1882, 'The Cowper Arms' was a temperance hotel and coffee house on Cheapside to provide workers and residents with an alternative to the public houses of the area. It was constructed in the Queen Anne Revival style with a

The former Cowper Arms, once a temperance hotel and coffee house.

jettied upper floor, triple gable and oriel windows with fine-shaped aprons beneath. It was run by the Beds Coffee Co. and was occupied in the early twentieth century by straw hat manufacturers. It was eventually to become a nightclub and today is a day care centre.

26. Bute House (formerly Bute Hospital)

Although Wardown House was opened as a military hospital for wounded troops, hundreds of soldiers were still treated along with civilians at the Bute Hospital in Dunstable Road during the First World War, greatly adding to its workload. In the three months up to September 1914, for instance, 269 patients had been treated, 142 of them soldiers billeted in Luton for only six or seven weeks. The extra fees paid by the military, plus £142 raised by some of the troops themselves, were beneficial to the Bute's finances, however, allowing equipment such as much-needed up-to-date X-ray equipment to be purchased.

The Bute Hospital was made possible by the gift of land in Dunstable Road by the Marquis of Bute in October 1879 and public fundraising. The new hospital opened on 27 September 1882 and replaced the small Luton Cottage Hospital, which opened in High Town Road on 6 May 1872, and for several years continued to carry the Cottage Hospital name.

Bute House, once a hospital and an important part of Luton's built heritage.

In 1902 it was decided to raise funds to build an extension with two new modern wards, costing £4,100. The new wards were opened on 2 July 1904 by Mrs Wernher of Luton Hoo. Another scheme of reconstruction started in 1910, leading to the opening of an extension on 8 July 1912 that included a new operating theatre at the rear.

The Bute continued to be Luton's principal hospital until 1939 (there was also the workhouse Infirmary, renamed St Mary's in 1929) when the new purpose-built Luton and Dunstable was opened on 14 February by Queen Mary. Work on the new hospital had begun on 31 March 1937, and the foundation stone was laid on 28 June that year. It was built on a 10-acre site at the junction of Dunstable Road and Lewsey Road, purchased in 1934 from Electrolux for £3,800.

27. Hibbert Cottages Almshouses

Robert Hibbert Junior (1769–1849) was the son of John Hibbert (1732–69) and Janet Gordon (1740–79). The couple had seven children and Robert was the youngest. Robert was a pupil of Gilbert Wakefield at Nottingham during the years 1784–87. Wakefield was a Unitarian and had worked in several Dissenting academies including Warrington Academy. He was politically a controversial figure whose pamphlet supporting the French Revolution landed him in prison

Hibbert Cottages Almshouses.

for two years in 1801 on a charge of sedition. Robert sent him £1,000 whilst he was incarcerated and the two men shared a close friendship. Robert attended Emmanuel College Cambridge between 1787–90 and was awarded a BA in 1791. In order to receive the BA Robert would have been compelled to subscribe to the established Church of England. At Cambridge Robert struck up a lifelong friendship with the radical and later Unitarian William Frend.

In 1791 Robert left England for Jamaica to take his place in the mercantile house founded by his uncle Thomas (1710–80) at Kingston. Robert returned to England in 1803 and became a partner in the Hibbert family's West India counting house. The West India merchant house was involved with the shipping, insurance and distribution of colonial commodities (particularly sugar). They owned their own ships and were also involved with finance and credit.

In 1806, he purchased an estate in Bedfordshire called East Hyde. Robert became High Sheriff of Bedfordshire in 1815. In January 1819 Robert paid for twelve cottages in Castle Street, Luton, for twenty-four 'poor widows or other persons' as well as funds for their maintenance. Later, Mrs Ashton's Charity of Dunstable, owners of the land behind these properties, wishing to undertake new building and gain frontage on Castle Street, negotiated with the trustees to demolish the old cottages and in exchange built new almshouses in 1885 by architect Alfred Williams on a new street off Castle Street, to be called Hibbert Street.

Unitarianism played an important role in Robert's life. In 1847 Robert executed a deed conveying to trustees $50,000 in 6 per cent Ohio stock, and £8,000 in railway shares. The trustees appointed alongside Robert were Mark Philips, MP for Manchester, and his brother Robert, both of whom were Robert's cousins.

Opened in 1884 based on designs by architect Alfred Williams.

He stipulated that the income should be spent 'in such manner as they in their uncontrolled discretion shall from time to time deem most conducive to the spread of Christianity in its most intelligible form, and to the unfettered exercise of the right of private judgement in matters of religion'. The Hibbert Trust is still in existence today and awards grants in line with Robert's wishes.

28. Former Hat Factory, No. 64 Bute Street

The Walter Gurney & Son Hat Factory on Bute Street, at No. 64, was built in 1889 and has an especially fine façade with pink-granite pilasters and stone detailing used here in contrast with the red brick. The building is finely enriched with stone mullions, transoms, architraves, cartouches and swags, all contributing to the enriched frontage of this building. Such ostentatious buildings as the

The former hat factory at No. 64 Bute Street.

one we find here were part of a trend in the late nineteenth century as the hat industry was expanding towards more accomplished designs. These buildings included decorative motifs and were visually more impressive and were intended to be more eye-catching. They were often located on busy thoroughfares. Their architects, builders and factory owners experimented with a wide variety of designs including polychromy, Queen Anne Revival and neo-Jacobean. Examples were many and included the Walter Gurney Building located here as well as others on Guildford Street. The Gurney building is a fine contrast to the more simplistic design opposite of the Connor building, now The Hat Factory with its upper floors in the Dutch style but the ground floor more classical. The Corinthian columns are echoed inside the building by cast-iron ones, which help support the structure. On the striking timber paneling of the entrance doors and surround and the etched-glass panels are the markings 'warehouse' and 'showroom'. The building is now Grade II listed.

29. Former Liberal Club, Nos 11 and 13 Manchester Street

The building on Nos 11 and 13 Manchester Street was built *c.* 1890 as the Liberal Club in a debased Jacobean style and is a standout building on this row. With its strong nonconformist background and its industrial interests, Luton was very solidly Liberal in its sympathies. The first member was Cyril Flower, who was a Liberal and who held the seat in the general election of 1886 when the Liberals were split on the Home Rule question, and again in 1892. He then went on to the House of Lords, where he became Lord Battersea. He was incredibly popular and was the first Honorary Freeman of the Borough, and even once in the House of Lords maintained a strong interest in Luton affairs.

However, it was the 1895 election that was to become the town's most exciting election. The Liberals lost heavily across the country and as the issue of drink and alcohol was the chief issue, the contest in Luton was hotly contested. The Liberal candidate T.G. Ashton won by a very narrow margin and the declaration of the result was followed by a serious riot that began with the breaking of windows across the town. Order was restored by the arrival of the Metropolitan Police, which quickly cleared the town, but many Lutonians had to spend the night in the fields afraid to return. Ashton was again returned in the election of 1900, when the country was divided and the same again in 1906 and 1910. Ashton was created Lord Ashton of Hyde after winning five successive elections.

One surprising choice of the Liberals was Cecil Harmsworth, who was the brother of Alfred Harmsworth, the founder and owner of the *Daily Mail*, the most extreme of the Conservative newspapers. Harmsworth convinced the local Liberals of his faith in their cause and was elected in the by-election of 1911. The war was soon to intervene and after the war, Labour was to appear with trade union membership growing. Over the following years, the seat was hotly contested

The former Liberal Club, almost overshadowed by the nearby Town Hall.

between Labour, the Liberals and the Conservatives. It was the Labour Party who had managed to build up a small but effective group on the town council. It was during this period that elections for the council were to be fought for the first time on a party basis.

The building on Manchester Street is a distant reminder of the days Liberalism ruled in Luton.

30. Former Hat Factory, No. 50 Guildford Street

With architects and factory owners experimenting with more ostentatious designs – as seen on Bute Street – along Guildford Street similar buildings were being erected. However, despite their magnificent frontages, there was often a more utilitarian side or rear to the building, indicating that greater expense was only reserved for their grander frontages. This is most apparent at the former nineteenth-century plait Durler & Suter warehouse at No. 50 Guildford Street. Its façade is very much in a Queen Anne/Jacobean style and dates from *c.* 1900 and is highly decorated in red-brick, terracotta and stone dressings, characterized by the use of a shaped gable flanked by volutes, containing a terracotta roundel with prominent voussoirs and with terracotta swags and tympana above many of the windows. Its side and rear though are much more basic in design and use of materials. The building is now also Grade II listed.

The former hat factory,
No. 50 Guildford Street.

Above: The stunning façade of No. 50 Guilford Street.

Below: The Queen Anne/Jacobean style of one of Luton's best-preserved former hat factories.

31. Bailey Hill Water Tower and Hart Hill Water Tower

In the Victorian period, Luton had begun to grow significantly. In 1841, its population was 5,827; by 1901 it had risen to 36,404. With that growth came a need for elements of urban infrastructure. The once navigable Lea had dwindled, within the town (but not downstream), to a small river, and was inadequate as a water-supply. Reliance was placed on wells at various locations. Against a degree of opposition, a piped water system was planned by the Luton Water Company, incorporated in 1865, although its first meeting was not held until 21 April 1868. A deep well was established in Crescent Road, close to the town centre, together with offices and a residence for the company's engineer.

In 1898, the water supply was badly affected by a serious drought, and as a consequence the several wells in Luton Rural District were deepened. But in the (then) outlying village of Stopsley (as elsewhere) the wells ran dry. 'Two 1.000 gallon water carts had to be brought up ... each evening at a cost of 3s. 8d. a cart'; it was also found that 'sewerage had seeped into some of the storage tanks and any water left was too filthy to drink'. Urgent consideration was given to the need to avoid such inconvenience and danger as a consequence of any future droughts. The solution adopted was to erect two water towers on high ground, one on either side the river, in then unbuilt areas: on Hart Hill (or Harthill) and on West Hill (also called Bailey Hill). Water was pumped from Crescent Road and stored in capacious tanks in the towers, whence it could be distributed by gravity.

Bailey Hill Water Tower, from Luton Hoo Memorial Park.

Luton Hoo Memorial Park.

Above: Bailey Hill Water Tower, converted into a residential property. What a view from it.

Below: Bailey Hill Water Tower, built in 1901.

Built in 1901 in the style of the Arts and Crafts movement, the Bailey Hill Water Tower was designed by Henry T. Hare. He was the architect behind the Oxford Town Hall and Fulham Library, and served as design consultant on Bailey Hill. It was built to supply water to Stopsley after the drought of 1898 but was decommissioned in 1960.

Built of Luton grey bricks with stone dressings, it is set on a square plan on splayed plinth with stone mouldings and rounded demi tower at each corner, the north-west one forming a stair tower with narrow slit casement windows. Pevsner described this building as 'one of the most enjoyable buildings of Luton ... decidedly Arts and Crafts and resourcefully handled'.

Recently converted, the property is now set over six floors and has four bedrooms, with an additional mezzanine level and a lift connecting all of the floors, in addition to the original stone staircase that still runs through the tower. In 2013, it was priced to sell at £1.5 million.

Also built in 1901 is the Hart Hill Water Tower. It is constructed of Luton grey bricks with red- brick dressings and particularly attractive terracotta decoration. Octagonal plan, it is four storeys high with a conical roof, deep projecting eaves, and surmounted by a finial. The roof of the main tower has four gables near the apex and four gabled dormers set lower down in the roof. One of the finest details of the building is the decorative terracotta frieze below the eaves. It was once described by the County Planning Department as like 'a French Gothic Chateau or a Chinese Pagoda'.

The Hart Hill Water Tower.

Almost like a Chinese pagoda, the Hart Hill Water Tower.

32. Bury Park United Reform Church

Bury Park is where Dunstable Road meets Leagrave Road. It takes its name from Bury Farm, which was near to where Kenilworth Road is now. An estate was built on the farm fields and the first houses were occupied in 1882. Church school halls were opened in 1895, and Bury Park United Reformed Church was built in 1903 and the Luton Industrial Co-operative Society Ltd opened its general store at the Dunstable Road/Leagrave Road intersection in 1906.

Before moving to its present ground in Kenilworth Road, Luton Town Football Club played home games on a field that became the site of the Odeon cinema (1938–83), which was later a bingo club and is now a church. The character of Dunstable Road altered with the coming of trams in 1908. Houses were turned into shops and their front gardens became paved forecourts.

The United Reform Church remains an important building in Bury Park. It was designed and built between 1895 and 1903 by G. Baines in neo-Decorated and Perpendicular style, on a corner site in a fine light red brick, with stone dressings and slate roofs. The schoolroom to the east was built first, followed by the cruciform church with a cambered tower on corner, short spire and weathervane. It was built to serve the residents of the rapidly expanding estate being erected on the fields of Bury Farm. Today the church can serve for a seated congregation of 600 people, with the pews being arranged in a semicircle around the pulpit and in a gallery at the rear.

Above: Bury Park United Reform Church.

Right: The tower of Bury Park United Reform Church.

33. Former Hat Factory, No. 40 Guildford Street

Overlooking Guildford Street is the rather bold design of the former hat factory of Henry Durler and Son, which was built in 1905 but using a cast-iron frame and a panel façade. The building was designed with several neo-Jacobean elements, which included the impressive obelisks either side of the gable, and is one of the tallest buildings in the area. The white-painted façade is crowned by a complex gabled parapet behind which is a truncated pyramid turret that may once have supported a flagpole. The building is especially notable for its use of a two-storey showroom front, with a giant arcade encompassing the half basement as well as the raised first and second floors, serving to distinguish the showroom and offices from the functional factory element on the floors above. It also included a number of Queen Anne Revival touches such as the swags above the attic window.

Former hat factory at
No. 40 Guildford Street,
built in 1905.

34. Vauxhall Motors, Kimpton Road

Luton is famed for its many years of vehicle and car production right here in the town. Vauxhall Motors began car production in 1905, which lasted until 2002. The company that led to Vauxhall was founded in 1857 under the name Alex Wilson and Company. Alex Wilson was a pump and marine engine manufacturer who had big dreams about development and his portfolio.

Six years later in 1863 the company was bought by Andrew Betts Brown. He renamed it Vauxhall Iron Works and they began making cranes. By 1903 cars started to be manufactured.

The name Vauxhall has a strange origin. Fulk le Breant was granted land by King John and it was Breant's house by the River Thames in London that became known as Fulk's Hall, which was changed to Fawkes Hall, then Foxhall and finally Vauxhall.

Vauxhall Motors' connection to Luton began in 1905 when Vauxhall Iron Works wanted to expand and chose a 7-acre site in Kimpton Road right on the periphery of Luton. Luton offered a cheap power supply with neighbouring Luton Electricity Works and it also had a lot of surrounding land that made it very desirable. The company became known as Vauxhall Motors in 1907.

In 1916, the then company chairman, Mr Leslie Walton, explained that even more land had been purchased for further expansion of the company. He said,

The Vauxhall factory on Kimpton Road, now manufacturing commercial vehicles.

Kimpton Road offices, part of the Vauxhall complex.

'We hope to increase its output very considerably this year, for the benefit of the country as well as the company.'

During the First World War the whole of Vauxhall car output was being supplied to the war office and the Luton factory produced more than 1,500 D-Type models as staff cars, and it was in one of these cars that King George V visited the battlefields at Vimy Ridge in July 1917.

Following the end of the war the lack of demand for premium-type vehicles meant that Vauxhall Motors struggled to make a consistent profit and in 1925 the company was acquired by American automobile manufacturer General Motors. Over the next five years the company direction moved more towards producing lower-cost but still premium vehicles in an effort to appeal to a wider market.

The Second World War saw Vauxhall play a major part in the war effort. The Churchill tank was produced here and battle-damaged tanks came back for repair. Thousands of Bedford lorries were turned out at Kimpton Road including the magnificent QL, which was the company's first four-wheel drive vehicle. Military contracts were to occupy Bedford workers for years to come and it was boasted that you could find Bedfords all over the world. Women joined the workforce in the war, many transferring from Luton's hat industry. Sadly, thirty-nine people lost their lives when a German bomb hit the factory in 1940. The heavily camouflaged factory continued to be a target; a landmine destined for Vauxhall blew up the town's bus garage.

Vauxhall started out as a luxury car brand, but after the Second World War it turned its attention to the mass-market. Famously produced cars include the Vauxhall Viva, a small family car in 1963; the larger Vauxhall Victor; and the infamous Chevette and Cavalier of 1975. This was the heyday of Vauxhall with as many as 36,000 people working at Kimpton Road, which had been expanded by excavating the side of a chalk hill away to build AA block.

In December 2000, Vauxhall announced that car production in Luton would cease in 2002, and the last cars to roll out of the forecourt were a Vauxhall Vectra, along with its closely matched companion, the Zafira. It used to be said that when Vauxhall sneezed, Luton caught a cold. Most Lutonians will remember the Vauxhall holiday when the whole town was deserted, and many a toyshop benefited each Easter as workers received a handsome cash bonus as profits were shared out.

Car production continues today at Ellesmere Port in Cheshire, a plant that originally opened in 1962 making components to supply to the production lines in Luton, before car production began there also in 1964.

35. Kenilworth Road, Home of Luton Town Football Club

Kenilworth Road has been the home of Luton Town since 1905, having left their previous home at Dunstable Road after their landlord disposed of the site for housing at short notice. It did not take the club's directors long to find a new site with their first match on 4 September 1905. Originally known as Ivy Road, the new ground was to bring success as in their last season at Dunstable Road Luton had finished second from bottom, but in the first at Kenilworth Road, Luton finished fourth in the Southern League.

Since its original construction in 1905, the ground has undergone many changes. It was not until 1932–33 that attendances were first counted, and Luton Town's average home attendance was taken at 5,868. Kenilworth Road's capacity at this time was 25,000, so it was not deemed necessary to improve the ground. However, only three years later, on 25 April 1936, a match against Coventry City attracted 23,142 spectators – at that time a club record. It was therefore decided to renovate the stadium, which was already in disrepair, and work began at the end of the following season. The Kenilworth End terrace was extended, the Oak Road End received a roof and major work was done on the Main Stand. Following these steps, the ground was more in line with those of rival clubs, the capacity increasing to 30,000. The first ten years following Kenilworth Road's renovation saw average attendances of between 15,000 and 18,000 and attendances steadily increased.

Sadly, renovation of Kenilworth Road was neglected for the next two decades – financial difficulties and the club's ambitions to build a new ground meant that regeneration was unaffordable, and would also prove unnecessary should relocation occur. However, following the rejection of several potential sites for a new ground, the club finally turned their attentions back to the maintenance of Kenilworth Road. The first real modernisation of the ground came in 1973, with the first addition of seats at the stadium since the construction of the new main stand in 1922. A £1 million refurbishment was carried out in 1985 with the introduction of the controversial artificial turf, as well as the conversion of the ground to all-seater, which began a year later in 1986.

The David Preece Stand was erected in 1991, simply called the New Stand on construction. The final improvements to the ground came in 2005, when the conversion of the Kenilworth Stand was finally completed to bring the capacity to its present 10,356. The increasingly unpopular artificial pitch was removed during the summer of 1991, following the banning of such surfaces from English football.

Luton Town have been looking for a new ground since 1955 without success, but they are currently planning to relocate to Power Court to a 17,500-seater new stadium for 2020–21.

Kenilworth Road stadium – the current home of Luton Town FC.

Kenilworth Road – the club is hoping to relocate in the future.

36. Former Hat Factory, No. 37–39 Guildford Street

The scale and complexity of industrial premises in Luton increased dramatically towards the end of the nineteenth century and into the early decades of the twentieth. Many of these were rebuilds of pre-existing, smaller concerns but a lesser proportion were entirely new constructions and all are contemporary with the collapse of the home-grown straw-plaiting industry as well as the introduction of a reliable and cheap electricity source to the town centre. There are a number of very distinctive buildings notable for their sheer scale and the complexity of architectural motifs and styles that were incorporated. The earliest of these were built at the end of the 1880s and designed to catch the eye of traffic moving through the town or arriving by train. A close proximity to the train station was desirable as it enabled an easier transport of materials to and from the factories – this was clearly a prime consideration and there are many contemporary commentaries on the congestion caused by traffic attempting to deliver goods to the train station at the end of the day: indeed even in the late 1890s it was remarked that 'at the top of Bute Street all vehicles bound for the Great Northern Station form themselves into an imposing procession, which would be a fit subject for the cinematograph'.

The Walter Gurney & Son factory at No. 64 Bute Street (Building No. 28), the Balfour Hat Factory at No. 50 Guildford Street (Building No. 30), and

No. 40 Guildford Street (Building No. 33) epitomised this phase of confident expansion in the industry. All three buildings are situated close to the station and its goods yards, and each occupies the location of an earlier factory or building. Their form is fairly typical of factories built at this time, consisting of a basement and ground floor provisioned with large windows, a formal centrally placed entrance and a smaller passageway to the side. Above this there are three/four storeys plus attic creating a lively street façade in comparison with what had been built in the area previously. Huge effort has been expended in their design and construction with the use of brick and stone with pilasters and elaborate windows incorporating cartouches and moulded stone swags. Each is further embellished by a shaped gable with a roundel window or similar and additional decorative features.

This same focus on the provision of an architecturally striking street frontage is evident at all of the major factories built at the turn of the century and into the first decades of the twentieth century, but the most outstanding of these is that constructed for Austin & Co. in 1912 at No. 37–39 Guildford Street. The street façade is remarkable and complex, incorporating a diverse mix of

Former hat factory, Nos 37–39 Guildford Street, built for Austin and Co.

features, and it has no direct comparisons within the vicinity. The façade of nearby No. 23–25 Guildford Street is equally impressive, if less detailed, and affected by recent renovation work. As with many of the buildings here, the current property is an amalgamation and rebuilding of earlier structures, on this occasion domestic outworkers, and the building dates to *c.* 1910–20.

Smaller-scale hat factories and workshops mirrored many of the characteristics of the larger buildings and followed the same layout of large ground-floor windows with double-entrance arrangements. A number of these are notable for their use of banded rustication such as the straw plait merchants at No. 37 Guildford Street.

37. The Painters Arms, High Town Road

Past another 'cut-off' corner at No. 21 Havelock Road and the adjoining 1870s terrace with its attractive arched doors and windows is the Grade II listed The Painters Arms, where a small public house, which opened in 1865, was rebuilt as now in 1913. The building has many attractive period details but perhaps its main claim to fame lies in the marital career of Sylvia Hawkes, step-daughter of the tenant landlord in the 1930s and remembered for her beauty. She married the Earl of Shaftesbury's heir, Lord Ashley, after which she broke up the romance of Mary Pickford and Douglas Fairbanks, whom she later married. When this failed, she was married in turn to Lord Stanley of Alderley, Clark Gable and Prince Djordgazi. She died in 1977 aged seventy-three.

The Painters Arms.

38. Stirling House, Former Hat Factory, No. 30 Guildford Street

No. 30 Guildford Street (Stirling House) is another ex-hat factory, used at one stage by a bridalwear company and a number of other businesses. It is built in a contrasting 'neo classical' style and dates from 1919. Here the ground floor showroom was given a bow window set behind the columns. The rest of Guildford Street in this direction shows a similar story, with former hat factories either demolished, converted to other uses or still empty and awaiting new occupants.

No. 30 Guildford Street, with its use of concrete render on a rigidly geometric façade, is markedly different in style to all of the earlier properties in the area. It was erected in 1919 to a design by Basil Deacon, commissioned by W. G. Dunham & Sons, building contractors, and is a fine example of neoclassical commercial

Stirling House
at No. 30
Guildford Street.

Stirling House at No. 30 Guildford Street, another former hat factory.

design, where the marginally recessed metal-framed glazing panels create a light impression within a bold framework. The ground floor is remarkable in its monumentality with a central bow window framed by Doric columns. The use of paterae within the entablature and fascia, and the use of pilasters with plain capitals, complete with drops, are all neoclassical features much in vogue at the time. Designs for the building show that the façade was largely built as shown, the most obvious alteration being the rendering of the inner pilasters, which were designed as exposed brick – it is not clear when the change was made. The plans are annotated with the proposed room functions and are typical in their layout: the basement was to be used for storage; the ground floor had a showroom at the front with offices, stairs and the lift in the centre (repeated on each floor) as well as access from the side for delivery of goods and for visiting agents, with a room for the packing and receiving of goods to the rear; the first floor had a workroom to the front with stockroom to the rear; the second floor was to have a machine or hand blocking room to the front with a finishers' workroom to the rear; whilst the upper floor was designed to house the functions of blocking and stiffening. Such an arrangement made the best use of the space and light available within the building and enabled a logical flow of materials during production.

39. The Hat Factory, No. 65–67 Bute Street

The Hat Factory is, as the name implies, a former manufacturing centre for hats. It was once J&K Connor Ltd's hat factory on Bute Street, well-known straw hat manufacturers. It was built in 1927 and has a strong industrial aesthetic, with long banks of windows and large open floors, marking it out as a 'daylight factory'. It originally comprised of old and new premises; the new factory, with five floors, is, presumably, the building fronting Bute Street today. The ground floor, comprised of the old premises, consisted of a drying room, an office, and a cutting room.

The new factory, the building we see today, was made of brick with a stone front and of steel construction. Connor's were in place up until 1950 with

The hat factory, Nos 65–67 Bute Street, one of the few former hat factories that has a new lease of life.

The impressive façade of this former hat factory.

the building vacant in 1960. No. 65 was occupied in 1965 by James Jameson (Dunluce) Limited, clothing manufacturers, and No. 65–67 by J. Albert & Company Limited, hat manufacturers, and Jo'Sella Limited, wholesale milliners (factory). Both were in occupation for the next ten years when the building became vacant again and in 1998, No. 65–67 Bute Street was a new arts and media centre called Artezium; it had still been a hat factory as late as the early 1990s, having last been occupied by a firm called James Egleton Limited. It is now an arts venue called, appropriately, The Hat Factory, which opened in 2003 and provides a mixture of contemporary theatre, dance and music.

40. Paul Walser's Former Hat Factory, Midland Road

Paul Walser was a Swiss national who died at the age of eighty-nine in September 1957. Although publicity shy, he had a keen eye for business and extended his connection with the country for which from the earlier days of his business career he had had a 'sneaking regard'. In 1906, he packed his bag and came over to London, where he founded the firm Paul Walser & Co. Ltd. Apart from straw goods plaits, he also started manufacturing ladies' hats. He was to meet significant local opposition with his latter undertaking, especially from

A former hat factory but blighted by an addition at the upper level.

old-established English houses that had formerly supplied him with plaits, and being a foreigner in addition, untold difficulties were put in his way. Undaunted by these obstacles, and with great perseverance, coupled with remarkable business ability, he succeeded in establishing a large concern, manufacturing 'Reslaw' hats (Walser backwards), which enjoyed a reputation all over the world. The firm of Paul Walser & Co. Ltd was to occupy their own premises consisting of nine floors in one of the great fashion centres of London, with additional workrooms nearby, and significantly they also owned a large factory here in Luton employing several hundred workhands.

The tall building curving on the corner of Midland Road and Old Bedford Road was built in 1929 as Paul Walser's hat factory (date is inscribed above the central second-floor window). Elegant and large windows are set between brick pilasters and the main entrance has a stone-effect 'classical' appearance with steps up to the door. It became known as Chiltern House, then became government offices but has more recently been redeveloped with very unsympathetic upper floors added and is now used as offices.

41. Denbigh High School, Alexandra Avenue

A number of new schools were built by Luton in the interwar years to meet the needs of the growing town and these included Denbigh Road, Maidenhall Road, Hart Lane and Beechwood Road. There were significant changes made at the existing Modern School, which by 1919 had grown so large that it was thought necessary to separate the boys from the girls. A school was started for girls in Alexandra Avenue, built in the 1930s in neoclassical style. The boys continued to be schooled in Park Square. Denbigh High School is an impressive building built of red brick with stone dressings, with a long main façade of twenty-five window bays.

Today, the school is a thriving community with over 1,000 pupils.

Denbigh High School with its long façade.

42. Church of St Andrew, Blenheim Crescent

The imposing Church of St Andrew stands in Blenheim Crescent. Its origins lay in the need to have a church presence in the Crawley Road area as Luton expanded north from the town centre. The idea was first raised in the 1880s when the area formed part of the parish of Christ Church, itself a relatively new parish, created in 1861 from the ancient parish of Saint Mary's.

The first record of a church here is in a record book beginning in 1887, which stated, 'The work begun September 26th: finished November 16th.' This is presumed to refer to the church erected in Gas Works Passage, on land donated by John Sambrook Crawley of Stockwood. It was a simple, corrugated iron structure and opened for worship as soon as it was completed.

By 1904 suggestions were being made that the church should be moved further north and of making it a more permanent structure. The Bishop's Commission of 1912–13 indeed recommended 'a new mission room for Saint Andrew's'. The congregation moved to a new site in Biscot Road in 1920, but the church still met in a temporary building – a war surplus army hut. The site was said to be 'in the cornfields'. Another hut was purchased two years later for the expanding congregation.

In May 1926 the Diocesan Board of Finance offered £5,000 to build a permanent church provided the parish of Christ Church could come up with

Church of St Andrew's on Blenheim Crescent.

Church of St Andrew's, a relation of Liverpool Cathedral.

a matching sum before the end of June 1931. A site was found at the rear of Alexandra Avenue in 1926. It was purchased from Luton Suburban Estates Limited, then being conveyed to the Diocesan Board of Finance in trust for the Parochial Church Council.

In fact, the foundation stone was laid on 28 July 1931 and the church was then built to the plans of Giles Gilbert Scott, architect for Liverpool Cathedral and Battersea Power Station, and overseen by Arthur W. Oakley. The completed church was consecrated on 23 October 1932.

The church is built of brick and is noted for its massive tower and big, sloping buttresses. Charles McKean noted that the church 'impresses by its sheer grandeur inside as outside'. It is certainly a memorable structure.

43. Blue Rails, Old Bedford Road

'Blue Rails', Luton's historic art deco house on Old Bedford Road, is a three-storey five-bedroomed house which was featured at the Ideal Home Exhibition in the 1930s. It was commissioned by the Dillingham family, who were owners of one of Luton's largest hat factories. It was designed by architect Charles Evelyn Simmons to incorporate as much sunlight as possible and was called the Sunway House. It was offered for the then princely sum of 1,100 plus 260 guineas for the solarium.

Blue Rails, designed by Charles Evelyn Simmons, renowned for his art deco buildings.

44. Luton Town Hall

Luton Town Hall is an example of interwar municipal architecture and was built between 1935–36 by architects Bradshaw Gass and Hope from Bolton. It retains much of its original detail despite alterations and additions in *c.* 1960. The design for the Town Hall was selected by competition, for which there were eighty-six entries in 1930. The previous town hall dated back to 1847 and was burnt down as a result of the Peace Riots of 19 July 1919, based on resentment directed at the council of the time. The original building was also owned by a private firm, the Town Hall Company. By 1876 Luton had gained the status of municipal borough and the new council took ownership from the Board of Health, which had bought the Town Hall the previous year.

The new town hall building was specifically designed to create a 'powerful and highly visible landmark' in the centre of the town, which it achieves admirably.

Luton Town Hall and War Memorial.

Above: The most prominent landmark building in Luton is the Town Hall.

Left: The magnificent Portland stone frontage of Luton Town Hall.

The 144-foot-high clock tower of Luton Town Hall.

Built of Portland stone facings to brickwork, and with ashlar carved decoration, it is of neoclassical style with art deco detailing. It is an iconic building in the centre of town primarily because of its 144-foot clock tower, which incorporates the coat of arms of Luton Borough Council. The Town Hall was eventually opened by the Duke of Kent on 28 October 1936, over seventeen years after the destruction of the previous building. Adding to the grandeur of the townscape, there is also the addition of the war memorial which commemorates the fallen from the First World War and was unveiled by Lady Ludlow on 10 December 1922.

45. London Luton Airport

London Luton Airport was officially opened on 16 July 1938 by the Right Honourable Kingsley Wood, Secretary of State for Air. The airport was owned by the Borough of Luton and was thought of as the northern terminal for London.

During the war, the airport was a base for 264 Fighter Squadron as well as a manufacturing site where both civil and military aircraft were designed and built. In 1952, civil use of the airport resumed and a new control tower was opened.

During the next ten years the 'package' holiday was developed and became very popular, allowing many people to travel abroad for the first time. Luton Airport played an important role in the development of the package holiday business in the UK. The formation of Euravia in 1962, now Britannia Airways, one of the world's largest charter airlines, was key to this development.

By 1969, a fifth of all holiday flights from the UK departed from Luton Airport and by 1972 Luton had become Britain's most profitable airport. However, when in 1974 the major tour operator Clarksons and its airline Court Line went into liquidation, Luton was hit hard. The airport was still recognised as an integral part of the London airports system though, and in 1978 the committee began preparations to take Luton into the future and raise passenger levels to 5 million a year. In 1985, a new international terminal building was opened by HRH The Prince of Wales.

The year 1986 saw Monarch Crown Service launch scheduled flights to Spain and Irish airline Ryanair launch scheduled services from Luton to Ireland. In 1987 Luton International Airport became a Limited Company with Luton Borough Council as sole shareholder. The airport was renamed London Luton Airport in 1990 to mark its position as part of the London airport network, but decline in passenger numbers struck again in 1991 as Ryanair moved a large part of its business to Stansted Airport.

The control tower of London Luton Airport.

In 1991, an unsuccessful attempt was made to sell the airport and a new management team was appointed to stop the losses and try and improve passenger numbers. Over the next five years £30 million was invested in the airport infrastructure and facilities were significantly improved. As a result of this investment, business increased during this period with the introduction of Airtours flights and the low-cost scheduled airlines Easyjet and Debonair. Passenger levels increased rapidly with 3.4 million in 1997–98 and rising again to 4.4 million by 1998–99, making London Luton the UK's fastest-growing major airport.

An £80 million development programme was completed in autumn 1999, giving the airport a £40 million terminal with sixty check-in desks. The airport continued steadily growing and in 2014 the airport reported record numbers of passengers, with over 10 million people flying from the terminal. In the same year, a major redevelopment plan was launched to redesign the terminal and ensure a smooth and easy experience for visitors to the airport. The revamp seems to have worked as by 2017 passenger numbers had increased to a record-breaking 15.7 million.

Luton Airport, continuing to modernise with new hotel complexes.

46. Former Bingo Hall and Odeon Cinema, No. 127 Dunstable Road

This unusual building was built for Oscar Deutsch's Odeon Theatres Ltd. The Odeon Theatre opened on 12 October 1938 with Sabu in 'The Drum'. The building is located away from Luton town centre in the Bury Park district and was designed by architect Keith P. Roberts of the Andrew Mather practice. The building is a rare example of thoroughgoing International Modernism applied to a cinema. The auditorium is a good example of the best streamlined style of the time, but the façade is a remarkably sophisticated piece of purist geometry, entirely lacking historicist references or even art deco styling. Keith Roberts (1910–94) was at the time the outstanding designer of International Modern cinemas in Britain, and the former Odeon here in Luton is the best remaining example.

With its entrance covered in cream tiles, it had an unusual tower feature, which still remains. The auditorium ran parallel to Dunstable Road and was a plain brick block, relieved only by ten vertical bands of brick and cream tiles at the lower lever. Inside, the decoration was streamline, with bands of concealed lighting on the ceiling of the auditorium. It provided seating for 1,332 in the stalls and 626 in the circle. The cinema also had a café for the convenience of its patrons.

The Odeon was converted into a triple-screen cinema in November 1974 and closed on 4 June 1983, screening *Local Hero*, *Tootsie* and *Silver Dream Racer*. The building was de-tripled and converted into a Top Rank Bingo Club, which

Almost ignored as part of Luton's built heritage, the former Odeon cinema on Dunstable Road is a rare example of international modernism applied to a cinema.

opened in July 1983. It was later renamed Mecca Bingo, which led to protests from the local Muslim population in the town, who assembled outside the building, smashing windows. Under pressure, the name 'Mecca' was removed from the front of the building, although it was retained inside. The bingo operation closed in late January 1999 and the building was given a Grade II listed building consent by English Heritage in March 1999.

It sat empty and unused until it reopened as the Calvary Church of God in Christ on 9 February 2001.

17. Former Cinema, No. 51 George Street

An unusual building is located at No. 51 George Street which is first listed in a directory of 1869 when it was in the occupation of Henry Gates, ironmonger and grocer. Gates is first listed in George Street in 1864 and may well have been in the same premises. Henry is last listed in 1877 and by 1894 William Lee Gates, ironmonger, grocer and 'agent for A. Gilbey Limited, wine and spirit merchants', is listed at the address. He was last listed in 1914 and by 1920 the occupier was F. W. Woolworth and Company, 'bazaar'.

William Lee Gates still owned No. 51 George Street in 1928 and leased the building to F. W. Woolworth and Company, who paid rent of £350 per annum.

A sign of troubled times – an empty building on George Street, once an important cinema in Luton town centre.

Woolworth is last listed in *Kelly's Directory* for the county of 1936. By 1939 the Savoy Cinema was at No. 51 George Street. By 1965 it had changed its name to the ABC. The building remains but is no longer a cinema.

C. G. Peck, in a 1981 booklet for Bedfordshire County Council on the history of Bedfordshire cinemas, wrote that the Savoy opened on 17 October 1938, the same week as the Odeon cinema at No. 127 Dunstable Road (Building No. 46). The cinema seated around 2,000 people and ABC Cinemas was the name of the owning company. It was still open at the time the booklet was written and then had three separate cinemas in one building. The first film shown was *Test Pilot* starring Spencer Tracey and Clark Gable. Midnight matinees were introduced in 1948 in an effort to bring in more customers. Today the building is boarded up and in poor condition.

48. The Arndale Centre, Mall and Central Library

The first step in the redevelopment of Luton town centre was the construction of the new Central Library on Bridge Street. Planning began as early as 1958, with visits to Swedish libraries in 1959 helping to form the final design. The library opened to the public on 24 September 1962 and featured many striking design features, both internally and externally, including the charming 'Story Hour Room' designed to look like the chamber of a castle set above the River Lea. Visited by the Queen and Prince Philip on 2 November 1962, the design was generally well received with the notable exception of Sir Albert Richardson (the past president of the Royal Academy), who felt it looked too like a factory and stated that 'I feel repelled by it ... it has a chilling effect which is very detrimental... People have lost the art nowadays of planning to a pattern.'

In the centre of Luton is the Arndale Centre, which was originally opened in 1972 as The Arndale Shopping Centre, providing the town (at that time) with the largest undercover shopping centre in Europe. It was ultimately purchased by Capital & Regional in January 2006. Like many developments in Luton over the years, many notable buildings were destroyed as a result of the building of the new shopping centre. Buildings that had survived the Second World War failed to survive the tide of progress – although many would argue this was progress at a cost. The area that would become the new shopping centre was ultimately cleared during the 1960s.

Further larger extensions were added to The Mall which would see total redevelopment of Silver Street, Bute Street, one side of Cheapside and part of Guildford Street, resulting in the demolition of further Grade II listed buildings and a number of former hat factories for which Luton was once so famous for but which resulted in criticism from English Heritage and the Victorian Society. In 2019, there are 158 retailers serving a catchment area of nearly 250,000 people with 900,000 square feet of retail space.

Above: Many historic buildings were demolished to make way for the 'progressive' Mall and Arndale Centre development.

Right: The Mall.

Above: The rear of the Mall and an atrocious example of town planning that is dominated by concrete and has no humanistic scale at all.

Below: Luton Central Library and Theatre.

49. Luton Central Mosque, Westbourne Road

Muslims have been worshipping at Westbourne Road in Luton since the 1970s. The initial site for the masjid was No. 2 Westbourne Road. As the Muslim population significantly grew in Luton, No. 4 and subsequently No. 6 were also acquired. The site was used for the five daily prayers as well as Jumu'ah Salah. Evening classes for children also took place to teach basic Arabic and Qur'anic studies. Larger gatherings such as the Eid prayers and Mawlid conference were difficult to accommodate as attendees would be scattered across three separate buildings. In the early 1980s the local community took a brave decision to

Luton Central Mosque.

and De Montfort University's Bedford campus. The Luton campus is located in the town centre and is home to a magnificent postgraduate and CPD Centre, a modern student campus centre and other excellent facilities such as the Media Arts Centre and Learning Resources Centre, creating an array of modern architecture in Luton town centre.

The University of Bedfordshire Luton campus.

Further Reading

Cook, Robert, *Around Luton* (Frith Book Co. Ltd, 2001).

Cook, Robert, *Luton Past and Present – The Changing Face of the City & Its People* (The History Press, 2013).

Cooper, Ken, *Luton Scene Again* (Phillimore, 1990).

Dyer, James; Stygall, Frank; Dony, John, *The Story of Luton* (White Crescent Press Ltd, Luton, 1964).

Luton Borough Council, *Luton's Heritage – Buildings of Architectural and Historic Interest* (Luton Borough Council)

Smith, Stuart, *Britain in Old Photographs – Luton - A Second Selection* (Sutton Publishing Ltd, 1996)

Stubbs, Mark, *Luton, The Archive Photographs Series* (Luton Borough Council, 1997).

White, Harold, *Luton Past and Present* (White Crescent Press Ltd, Luton, 1977).

White, Harold, *Luton – A Collection of 145 Pictures* (White Crescent Press Ltd, Luton, 1974).

http://bedsarchives.bedford.gov.uk/ArchivesAndRecordOffice.aspx

http://www.lutonheritageforum.org/index.html

https://www.lutonhoo.co.uk/history-luton-hoo

About the Author

Paul Rabbitts is a Fellow of the Royal Society of Arts and a Fellow of the Landscape Institute. He is currently Head of Parks for Watford Borough Council and has worked in the public sector for over thirty years. He moved to Leighton Buzzard in 2011 and has been a prolific author on public parks, the royal parks, the Victorian bandstand and has extended his interest in local history to architecture, including biographies on Decimus Burton, Sir Christopher Wren and Grinling Gibbons. He has also written a number of books in the *in 50 Buildings* series for Leighton Buzzard, Watford, Windsor & Eton, Salford, and Manchester.